FINISHING LINE PRESS

www.finishinglinepress.com

Ponies and Other Poems

poems by

Cheryl A. Derby

Finishing Line Press
Georgetown, Kentucky

Ponies and Other Poems

ACKNOWLEDGMENTS

Thank you to Tonya Moutray for her review of my book and for having me
read my poems at Russell sage College.

Previous poems published in *Nimrod, Limestone, Confluence, Phi Kappa
Phi Forum, Riversedge, The Texas Review, Missouri Review,* and *Columbia
University.*

Publisher: Leah Huete de Maines
Editor: Christen Kincaid
Cover Art: Cheryl Derby
Author Photo: Cheryl Derby
Cover Design: Elizabeth Maines McCleavy

Order online: www.finishinglinepress.com
also available on amazon.com

Author inquiries and mail orders:
Finishing Line Press
PO Box 1626
Georgetown, Kentucky 40324
USA

Contents

Introduction

Ponies and Other Poems by Cheryl Derby aim to interpret a sense of place through horses, mice, rain, love, death, and the theme of adolescence searching for adulthood.

The magic mirror of poetry reflects all life and love. It seizes a moment and finds a way when other ways may hinder. Poetry is the magic mirror birthing us on, interpreting sorrow that turns to witness, leaps to temporary joy, flying into being. Breathing poems.

Ponies

"There are no angels hovering over me," she said,
cleaning up her messes.
Everyday she mopped,
then reached into the secret hiding place,
jangled some change.
"Money watches over me."

There are movements and counter movements;
what about reverse movements?
If only these greedy hands could give back time;
start again with its ticking,
start again with a lullaby.

And the ponies would ride
just a little bit smoother,
instead of the bucking,
I fell off every time.
And the ponies would ride in deep velvet,
to a lullaby.

Something in the air tonight,
a warm fair dark with ride,
filled with lullabies.

Sheets

Waves crash into the present,
fading to a past.
Mist; their ghostly presence

White sheets strain against the day's great weight.
Their purity confounds me.
You are a great weight or ghostly presence.

The white sheets are blank,
I cannot fill them in,
nor write you over.

Sheets, like naked strangers I don't know.
This is summer, its sea of strangers, sleeping under sheets.
Lovesick girl, blue bathing suit, walks amongst the sheets
at seventeen. Amongst the waves, the water closes in on what she
    knows.

Love, the shadow of her days, bright and dark.
Love, her jewels, jewel pressed to the hand, sapphires, golds wave
    round her
under sun's bare bulb,
great gulls, cry the world to foam.

Rain is a Stranger

Driving down backroads,
the rain rushing through woods,
trees' punctured by rain's kiss.
We, inundated, no town to get to.
The rain seeks another, pressing on.

It is on the verge of knowing.
A lonely beauty?
Its veil drops to silence,
to the drawn shade of a farmhouse.
Your radio crackles.
I am a stranger here,
I shall never catch up to you.

You are my farmhouse,
yes, keep my umbrella.
Into these holes, fill water.
They play upon the hour,
swept into a season., by leaves.
We gravitate towards the window.

You are all shadow, as night rushes on.
I am stranger beside you.
We live, skin soaked,
narrow stairwells we climb,
to tumble down, covered by leaves.

There, a small child inside, heard from again, stops, smiles.
We deafen each other with our thoughts.
We are on the verge of knowing.
But not yet.
Your radio crackles.
I kiss the air, hot with your breath.
This is how the rain aches in our arms,
world vanished for now.

Into Snow

Always carry a small bird in your pocket
for when you are bored, waiting for life to begin,
you can stroke its feathers of flight.

Remember the look of desire in your lover's eyes,
to keep from counting the days,
that like escalator steps glide into nothingness.

You can be a child,
when you clean up after yourself,
or your mother making you feel
small as a black dot on a blotchy night.

When you know less and less about the sky,
and where it is taking you,
you can be o.k. with a burning mattress,
as long as it's dragged into the snow.

You know you're not Julie,
her brown hair being tossed by the wind
in Fall's thickening mist.

Who is she speaking to?
Juliet inside of Julie.
Don't let morning take her.
Freeze her mirror,
the one I'm looking into.

Shredding leaves, crumble, take root.
Freeze our mirror. Old is this Autumn,
inflicted with an ancient heart.

Forever are the leaves dying,
caught by wind whirling.
This fullness of time forever.
where other's feelings matter.

I am emptied into a space,
as Fall has left.
I am stillness in this hush of snow.
Into this silence, I burn candles.
Into this dusk.

Into this hush, I am love-struck.
Fearing love.

Is it so struck with light?
so weightless in the snow?
I am as much as I'll ever be.
All his gestures ignite,
strong as stars.

Magic Mirror

Luxury is the desire of wanting you.
In the mirror of what happened,
your bittersweet leaves a stain on my mouth.

In between, we crawled twilights, in between, we dreamt of escape.
So, birds find a crack in the sky,
in the space of a heart.
So many gates to open, so many birds have landed,
the heart finds a space, if only till tomorrow.

Arms entwined; we climbed the hill.

Broken cottage, early or late,
your beads of wood and one of rain.
We slide into light.
You are gossamer man, whose twigs ignite.

You strike with an ax,
rend cracks in the sky.
Teach me a world, another world,
to find a pearl, our cottage.

Tonight, two trees in silhouette.
We stand, listen to the evening passing.
I listen to your day of cutting and sawing,
as you build a magic mirror.

Make us younger.
We are no different than anyone else.
We do not count time by clocks or hours descending.
but on fluttering notes, fluttering wings;
there clouds reflected in.

If our sun hung on for years,
there would be colored fruits the size of your generosity,
living in your magic mirror.

Dandelions

Full of seed stars, the dandelions burst open
to float like snow dreams over the field.
All night the seed stars blew
like a soft bliss waking something in me,
space for the wild things to incubate.

In compliant boughs,
that never still in his palms,
over the quarter horses, when stars tattoo the heart.
I woke to them unloosening the night.

Dizzy with gazing upwards,
night slipping like a shoulder strap,
the faint whinnying catching the air.
They were darkness, they were light,
never to be caught inside the stalls.

Barn becomes a distant itself,
where distance disappears in soundless gliding, past midnight.

The sky wears its warm damask.
Blond reeds meet the eyes, in the soughing that grows.
Love noses the air.

Make me small as a newborn mouse, close to earth.
The world cries out at night, filled with heart beat.

Litter of Snowflakes

Your sawdust shirts I wanted to clean.
They hang with my wilted dress, in the hour of dusk.
Such hurt like the window was cracking,
to let more room in with the sky.

Winter was a forest of arms holding us captive.
Our slow selves tooled to leather fellowship,
zipped up against the snow airs, in sculpted shadows.

Past snow's stump, logs chewed up,
tooth marked. We passed a cabin,
past the snowman. His heart beat.
His frozen face marked us as we crunched past.

Season wore dark airs of starkness.
We plunged past cave holes, litters of snowflakes fallen.
We dreamt the caskets of a lifetime, in between our love.

Prow

Night distracts me.
I'm tugged by these winds.
Here, there is no rest for statues,
Massive shipheads that sit in this room.

I came to him, as wooden,
Listing to his words,
Unable to understand.

He wanted to carve a statue,
A Helen, Thetis, the animalist
That wrestled in Pelia's hold,
From each winding post
that swirls and swivels.

His dream was his life.
Now his death, in the sea's culled shells,
The foam's hiss.
Ocean masses over, its own stone statues.

Through mirrors or swells,
I visit his house, now darkened, now in ruins.
I slide though wooden doors.
I am no longer wooden.

He is still learning to love me.
Death keeps our truth.

Brown Grass

He lived in his own fabric,
by moment's open end.
Dark is the schoolyard,
the browning grass now done.
It wanted to call back the birds,
it wanted nothing tied down.

It wanted the swollen moment,
the disturbance of summer,
to fix the dark sun.

The browning grass had a lover,
maybe a river, surely a lake.
The browning grass had a Blue Jay.

Maple, sugar maple,
the wind blew the pages of these many poems,
lost its place amongst the leaves.
Each breeze bloomed a freedom.
Luminosity is what the words say,
if the disturbance of summer drives Fall away.

To a dungeon in the rain,
dark the schoolyard.
I hear the Blue Jay, its rain bird screech
fill showers with words,
They may disintegrate in an ocean of flowers,
or blow to bits these poems,
forced to shreds by the wind.

The Stilled Birds

All day I watched the silvered trees shed icicles.
Diamond air pierced, then caught the world
until melting.

Birds sweep or chase.
They pause, all gesture, then tear into my wool coat.
I, exposed to black and white, freeze
chemicals settling, each shot of sky, I take,
trees chilled as my bones.

The walk this afternoon to find your name frozen into icicles.
As if my hot hands could melt your words, let the ink flow,
almost a river.

I'm remembering my mother writing her reckless book.
Snow closed her in, a gathering secret grew her divorce.
She wore a mask, separated by weather,
she wore the mask of other.

Human animal I was, tracking her.
She wore a mask of silhouette. Chiffon worlds loomed at her,
unknown. The snow closed in. I clicked the shot.
She wore a mask, pierced world of diamonds.

Sometimes, ink flows, almost a river.
Sometimes crows cry, always wordless.

Flickering

Language began in waves,
pushing forever away,
world happened, spider webbed.

I do not know this world,
or summer of measures, lines to draw
and the river stuck in a day.
Clay on the bottom, shellacked by water.

Day is a weight of heavy iron, of rusting stones.
Once I heard its music, gliding water snake,
smelled the poppies, roses and oranges of rain,
full of slapping leaves.

My voice was your voice,
echoing, as you skipped stones.
You skipped stones and
we flickered on and off, two lights.
We flickered further down
two fireflies through the night, then stumbled on,
two humans by the rock bed.

I wanted to make you a hero, where past and future never met.
But water moves on dragging its flowers.
River ripples at the edge, carries on.

Rose

In the mutilated light,
on the faceted trail to the hidden pond,
love-in-the-mist, cloud grass,
Yarrow to heal your hands,
encased in shimmering diamonds of rain.
Evergreens mirroring, ourselves everywhere in the drizzled earth.

Flowers open to rain, grasses and seeds.
Eternal love, picked green, in the rough places,
by childish fingers.
He has found a tree's hollow.

The burr stuck once and in my hair,
the pond a reflection of Mother.
She left her many gates open.
To mug wort, well it can be dried,
although found at demolition sites
and are attractive to mice.

I gave my mother heather, for good luck.
A small bouquet of that and rosebuds
make a gift for her, Rose, her name.
Picking times are July and August.

Buttonholes

Buttonholes of darkness fitted into the folds,
snow dropping in heaps to the naked earth,
these dresses of snow,
softening against sharp edges.

Night, she climbs to the precipice,
of hushed notes, there is landscape, seamless.

Cold burns a question in her throat
where truth runs rampant,
snow a lozenge, to suck on.

In the time of red carpets, we saw,
beyond frozen white heaps melting,
against factory candles (where he worked)
down the wax paper sky,
windows locked into bedroom.

The deep gold daughters burned through icicles,
breathing a poem.
There were others—some kids who explored the word never,
swapping forever.

Growing, we fly. We fly into being.
Their winding shirts, throbbing shirts softly struck.
Nymphs of the night.
Love, she puts on winter.

Memphis Corners

Outside the car, it rained so hard,
I couldn't breathe.

I ran into the bar and took a seat,
past tomato-colored barns,
cornstalks clothed in rain's sorrow,
crackling logs warming Memphis Corner's Bar.

Day came crashed to smithereens,
such thunder, dark markings slashed upon the wall.

Men huddled inside their scotches,
bursts of laughter beneath the gloom,
in between he almost cried.

Guitars boomed from the walls of water,
sometimes saying that we loved,
his boat of laughter pitched and tossed
on fickle seas.

In the holy land of their voices,
I search for the soul of this day.
In the wreck of rain,
Denice was his sky swallowing earth.

The drowned crowned roses
were everywhere for her,
the drowned crowned roses
heavy on the stool.
The air of this bar close,
closed on my throat.

Call the day corn,
rain that grew these ears,
now picked, gone.

He chased her though cornstalks
all summer long,
on the edge of my life.
I got tangled in the long grass,
in between, we almost cried.
Everywhere from her.

Chatty Kathy—The Believer

In case you were wondering,
my family went to Cancun
while I stayed home,
writing and painting to the bone
in my elbow, almost like cleaning,
these words I polish
a Windex for the mirror of the soul.

I am my glasses, in a glass reflecting
my blue journal, brown books,
red notebook.

I dream, very solid dreams
of what we never did in life.

The further the clock ticks down the hallway,
the closer I am to reaching your time.
Summer carved in stone, in minutes, hours,
Chatty Kathy believing in what she says.

My fearless, she says,
so many dreams of you as my life passes.
746 watts of horsepower behind my dreams,
with no horses in sight,
only eureka moments in the red morning light.
It tempers the day.

I will believe in you.
I shall be hurled by my string
into your liquid ways.

Birthday

Swift the current that carries me past you,
caught on the logs, under ripples of stumps,
tooth marked, chewed up, sawed down.
Wind, pocked and riled, churns up water.

I wanted to stay 39, live in a cabin you built,
see through a summer of red glass,
your flushed skin, to bury my face in,
those few good days.

Don't Touch

As leaves fall, there's a high wall
we can't see over.
Down the blind corridor,
soft tickings bring first frost,
first snow.

We fall into a well,
after climbing stairs,
cool hands smoothing over.
The secrets we keep,
our window filling with frost.

Don't touch.
We are virgin lilies.
We are snow made from heaven.
No time is wrong. Right now,
we float through distance,
we, flakes of snow.

We are heard opening the room,
soft as love in this dim sky.
Hard as a key unclicking the lock.

Locked into frozen sky,
viewed,
from everywhere, you, I
until we lose track of tomorrow.

Black Lake

Evergreens mirroring, ourselves everywhere
in the drizzled earth,
encased in shimmering diamonds of rain.
Out of the tentacle air,
clinging moistness of roots, fallen petals.

These forest of arms grope.
It is the hour of the sky.

Here was the red dust sunset, in its chemical wash,
becoming more than photo.
Moving vehicle of the sun, dropping
to silhouette toy trees
that cut the late orange sky.
The train blanks through so many miles to go.
Dusk has wound its way through these rockers.
I cannot be still, the baby will not hush.

It's not my child,
seeking colors of lime or strawberry.
Inner vision has become a strange child,
all darks beyond the horizon,
roads, crossings,
where a child never entered nor a stepchild.

Picture a lake; I am all reflections.
I listen to bodies of water,
this last, at Black Lake.

It almost sank with the deluge, all day into night.
When I woke, the camper awning was flapping through gales of
    wind.
I wanted to be taken then.
I cannot be still.
This baby will not hush.

Catacombs

I awoke from the deep place of catacombs.
The statues of winter were mounding,
white, each tree, each post, house.
The ghost flakes had ticked through sleep's lucidity,
heightening an awareness,
this fall of snow.

Morning is the cold wall risen,
morning is the vase,
the glass still with meaning.
I held it like a captured bell.

Inside frost of frozen flowers;
my hands bring rain to these flowers melting,
lost to silence.

To bring the speechless up to from the heart,
what had been frozen.
To utter father, childhood father,
or harder, childhood mother,
in this sphere wakening.

The statues whipped,
their beings dragged by wind,
snowdrifts like sand dunes, almost.

I make a diary of their changing shapes.
Trees, bushes,
sudden gaps of stones, half hidden, breaking ground.
Mother, Father, buried now.

Allan

Humid wind blows an oven of passion.
His hot breath mouths silent names.
Under the signpost,
obscured in dim light,
night stays cryptic in the roadside maples.

Their blackened bark promises.
We are fluttering, airborne in the art of happening.

The thrum of drumbeat beats what summer is,
hearts startled by song,
that weave into fences,
balanced there, hung
like the moon in its web.

Sticky with summer,
love is the night sliced open,
in shards of silver,
the red eye of fear, sleepless.

Carved are the wooden faces
of parents, under doors passed.
Music enters a space,
to make us familiar on this blown night.

When time suspends-
time expected to unfold;
breaks off like a stem from a rose.

And fills your small sketches,
laying on the floor.

Cheryl Derby was born into her family's book business. In her teens, she worked for her grandfather, and then at her mother's bookstore. Her father and grandfather owned The Economy Book and Stationary Store in Syracuse, N.Y.

After graduating from S.U.N.Y. Geneseo with a double major English and Art, she owned her own bookstore in the Albany-Troy area of N.Y. for many years. She also lived in the country during her teens. It was then she fell in love with nature and was greatly influenced by her many peers.

Cheryl is also a visual artist painting in watercolor, acrylic, pastel and oils. She's a member artist at Southern Vermont Art Center in Manchester, Vermont. Based on her life, a love passing early, her parent's passing recently, and a younger sister who passed in 2014 all became part of her poetry story.

Her grandfather's love for books led him to open many bookstores in the Northeast. Cheryl also worked in her grandfather's Book Warehouse where she worked with a variety of people, including a couple who lived in their car.

Her education included other lifestyles besides academia. Her peers in the country were also farmers and factory workers. She met all kinds of customers through her retail bookstore. At her mother's bookstore, she became inspired to write poetry with the wonderful selection of poetry books.